BUILDING THE WALL

Also by Robert Schenkkan

Hanussen
Shadowplay
The Kentucky Cycle
By the Waters of Babylon
The Marriage of Miss Hollywood and King Neptune
Handler
Conversations with the Spanish Lady and Other Plays
The Dream Thief
Heaven on Earth
Final Passages
A Single Shard
The Devil and Daniel Webster
All the Way
The Great Society

BUILDING THE WALL

THE PLAY & COMMENTARY

ROBERT SCHENKKAN

With Afterwords by
Timothy Patrick McCarthy,
Douglas S. Massey, and
Julian E. Zelizer

Arcade Publishing • New York

First Edition

Arcade Publishing books may be purchased in bulk at special discounts for sales
promotion, corporate gifts, fund-raising, or educational purposes. Special edi-
tions can also be created to specifications. For details, contact the Special Sales
Department, Arcade Publishing, 307 West 36th Street, 11th Floor, New York,
NY 10018 or arcade@skyhorsepublishing.com.

Arcade Publishing® is a registered trademark of Skyhorse Publishing, Inc.®,
a Delaware corporation.

Visit our website at www.arcadepub.com.
Visit the author's website at www.robertschenkkan.com.

*BUILDING THE WALL was first produced as a National New Play Network
Rolling World Premiere by The Fountain Theatre (CA), Curious Theatre Company
(CO), Forum Theatre (DC), Borderlands Theatre (AZ), and City Theatre (FL),
with support from Paul Prokop. For more information please visit www.nnpn.org.*

BUILDING THE WALL was developed at The Lark, New York City.

10 9 8 7 6 5 4 3 2 1

Library of Congress Cataloging-in-Publication Data is available on file.

Cover design by Brian Peterson
Front jacket photo: iStock

Print ISBN: 978-1-62872-877-4
Ebook ISBN: 978-1-62872-878-1

Printed in the United States of America

Contents

Author's Note on
Building the Wall

"The only thing necessary for the triumph of evil is that good men do nothing."

—Edmund Burke

What does a writer who has often turned to history to illuminate present political crises do when he finds himself living through a turning point in history? We are experiencing an extraordinary moment in the life of our republic, an unprecedented crisis created by an American version of authoritarianism that is waging an all-out attack on fundamental American values. This is not a partisan issue but a matter of concern to all of us. While I would like to be hopeful, the outcome is far from certain.

Several years ago, I stumbled across the book *Into That Darkness* by Gitta Sereny. It is an attempt to understand the bleakest of the Nazi horrors by focusing on one ordinary man who, for a brief moment, found himself with unlimited power. As someone whose family suffered grievous losses in the Holocaust, Ms. Sereny's account stayed with me, as did the lesson derived from it: if you do not pay attention, the unimaginable can become inevitable.

Then, in October of last year, as the most expensive and dispiriting presidential campaign in recent memory was coming to a close, I sat down and, in a white-hot fury, wrote this play. In it, I have imagined a not-so-distant future in which now-President Trump's racist campaign rhetoric on immigration and border security has found its full expression. While our current political crisis is extraordinary, it is not new—the authoritarian playbook is well-established. Create a constant state of crisis that only a "strong" leader can solve. Encourage fear, divide the populace, and scapegoat minorities with appeals to nationalism, racism, and isolationism. Smear your opponents as unpatriotic, and tell the press to "just shut up and listen." The question, of course, is not so much what the authorities will do, but how we, the citizens, will respond. Sickened by the hate, by the constant assault, will we succumb to our fears, avert our gaze, and look after our own interests? Will we enthusiastically put our shoulders to their dark wheel? Or will we resist? To those who say that it could never happen here in this country, I reply, maybe not, but that of course will depend entirely on what *you* do.

ROBERT SCHENKKAN
MARCH 6, 2017

BUILDING THE WALL

LIGHT/SOUND. A prison meeting room. El Paso, Texas. 2019. Two people stand facing one another, a heavy metal table between them. GLORIA is an African-American woman in her forties. Intelligent. Warm. Modestly dressed. RICK is a white man in his forties. He wears an orange prison jumpsuit.

GLORIA

You mind, you mind if I record? I'll also take notes but this allows me to be accurate.

RICK doesn't respond. GLORIA pulls a digital recorder from her bag and sets it up on the table.

RICK

I imagine we're both being recorded right now.

GLORIA stops and glances around.

GLORIA

Really?

RICK

And watched.

GLORIA

I think that's supposed to be for my safety.

RICK

Or mine. Kinda weird, when you think about it. They don't want me to kill myself so they can kill me. Are you worried about your safety?

SHE studies him a moment.

GLORIA

No.

RICK

But you're nervous?

GLORIA

Sure.

RICK nods.

RICK

I like that. That you're honest. That stood out in your letters.

GLORIA

I think if we're not honest, what's the point?

RICK

(*Nodding*)

I haven't met a lot of college professors before. Lawyers, yeah. Shrinks. But not— You don't look like what I thought.

GLORIA

How is that? You mean black.

RICK

I'm not allowed computer access so I couldn't look you up. I don't know what they think I'm going to do with a computer, you know, reach out to my huge fan base and incite a—

GLORIA

Is my race a problem for you?

A moment.

RICK

I never know what word to use. Black. African American.

GLORIA

I like black. Is it a problem, Rick?

RICK

It doesn't matter to me. I'm not racist. I've lived and worked with all kinds of people.

GLORIA

Hispanic?

RICK

In Texas, are you kidding? You could throw a rock in any direction and you'd hit one.
(*Beat*)
Unfortunate expression there.

GLORIA

Muslim?

RICK

Sure.

GLORIA

You have Muslim friends? Had Muslim friends?

RICK

I knew some but those people, they kinda stick together, you know.

GLORIA

But you had no personal animus against Muslims and Hispanics.

                              RICK

No.

                             GLORIA

And yet here you are.

                              RICK

Look, I'm not crazy, it was the situation. There was enormous pressure from the Brass and stuff just—

                             GLORIA

Rick, if you insist on repeating the same bullshit your lawyer
gave the court then I am going to walk out of here and never
come back. On the other hand, if you want to talk to me, one
person to another, really talk to me about what happened and
why, maybe help us all understand so that nobody else finds
themselves in your situation, then we can do that. But you
have to be honest with me. Can you do that? Can you just be
honest?

      A moment. GLORIA shrugs and starts to pack her things.

                              RICK

OK. OK.

      GLORIA stops and considers him.

                             GLORIA

I want to hear your side, Rick, in your own words. That's

why I'm here. If you're honest with me, I'll see that what you say is printed just like you say it. No filter. No editing. Your words.

SHE glances at the door.

GLORIA

They haven't given us a lot of time, Rick. And I don't honestly know if they'll let me come back after today.

A moment.

RICK

I don't, I don't have anybody to talk to in here.

GLORIA

You're in solitary, yes?

RICK

"For my own protection."

GLORIA

You sound skeptical.

RICK shrugs.

GLORIA

You think one of the other prisoners might try to harm you?

RICK

My experience has been, in certain situations people tend to act in their own interests.

GLORIA

There's value in your death?

RICK

Well, the government certainly seems to think so.

GLORIA

There's been no decision yet.

RICK

If you believe that, you're not nearly as smart as you think you are.
(*Quietly*)
I'm not talking about the courts. Justice. I saw things. I know stuff that would make a lot of people look bad.

GLORIA

That's why it's important we talk now. That your story gets told now before it gets changed into something else. Distorted. Revised.

RICK

And why are *you* here, professor? Out of your ivory tower. Purely for academic reasons? You're what, performing a social service? No thought for yourself? You didn't think, maybe, for just a second, about the possibility of a big book deal, future movie rights, awards, fame?

A moment.

GLORIA

I've thought about it, sure, but I can't say that's what drives me. I think this could be a book, yes. There's interest in you, certainly, in your story. I think it's very important. But maybe it's not a book, maybe it's an article. Or maybe at the end of the day I just go home and burn my notes.

RICK

In that case, what's the point in me talking to you?
  (*Beat*)
Why are you here?

A moment.

GLORIA

The first time I understood race in this country I was at a Fourth of July parade with my folks. They had put red, white, and blue ribbons in my hair and I was very proud of them. I was standing there on the corner, holding my mother's hand, my daddy had gone to get me a snow cone, and this policeman who was providing security looked over at me and smiled. I knew he was going to say something nice to me because that's what grown-ups did. And he leaned over and said to me very quietly, "Hello, little nigger, how are you doing today?" I was six.

(*Beat*)

I think it's fair to say that most black people don't spend a lot of time trying to understand racism so much as survive it. We're looking for the work-around, not the explanation. I'm a little bit different, maybe. I've thought a lot about that police officer. Was his racism so intrinsic to who he was that he wasn't even aware of it any longer? Or did he know exactly what he was doing and there was a special thrill in taking this black child's racial innocence? I started in psychology and moved into sociology but where I wound up was history. I look at the continuum of events and try to sort out those moments of change where often it is a single individual's decision to act or not to act that sends history spinning in this direction or that. We're at one of those moments right now. You're at the heart of it. I can't imagine— I think it's important, I think it's *critical*, to understand *you*. Understand why you did what you did.

(*Beat.*)

RICK

I didn't talk at trial, the only reason I didn't talk at the trial, was because my lawyer said I shouldn't.

GLORIA

Self-incrimination.

RICK

Not that it obviously made any kind of difference to the jury but the worst part was me sitting there all those weeks, listening to the bullshit being said and not able to respond.

GLORIA

So you want to clear the record. I get it. We can do that.

A moment.

RICK

Yeah. OK. So. It wasn't about race.

GLORIA

What was it about?

RICK looks away; seems uncomfortable.

GLORIA

Why don't you start by telling me about yourself, your family, growing up? Austin, right?

RICK

Born, yeah, but we moved a lot.

GLORIA

Why was that?

RICK

Military brat. Dad was Air Force.

GLORIA

Were you close?

RICK

(*Laughs*)
My dad? I don't think he was too big on family. He told me
I was a mistake. On more than one occasion. Mostly I tried
to stay out of his way.

GLORIA

He was abusive?

RICK

Well, that would be awfully convenient, wouldn't it? Wrap
this whole thing up in a nice tidy bow.

GLORIA

He never hit you?

RICK

Sure, of course he did. Rung my bell good a couple of times.

Nothing wrong with that. Discipline. You know, "Spare the rod."

GLORIA

Religious household?

RICK

My mom was a big believer. My dad, not so much. More of the Church of Budweiser.

GLORIA

He drank?

RICK

(*Flatly*)
This is Texas.

GLORIA

He had a problem?

RICK

Not when he was drinking! He liked a cold one at the end of the day; take the edge off. Or two or three. Not so different from most of the people I know. You drink, right?

GLORIA

I did, sure.

RICK

Not anymore?

GLORIA

Were you religious?

RICK

I went to service with my mom. Sunday school. Church suppers. They dunked me in the river when I was thirteen. The whole nine yards. It never really took though. It was just something you did and so I did it.

GLORIA

Would you say that's true of you in general? Go with the flow?

RICK considers her.

RICK

Don't get all excited, professor. Things are a bit more complicated than that.

GLORIA is a little surprised but smiles an acknowledgment.

GLORIA

Fair enough. OK.

                          RICK
OK.

                         GLORIA
Is it true you've become religious in here?

                          RICK
     (*Shrugging*)
I talk to the minister sometimes, yeah.

                         GLORIA
That help you?

     A moment.

                          RICK
Not so much.

                         GLORIA
So, you wouldn't exactly describe your father as abusive but
you left home when you were sixteen and stayed with your
grandparents.

     RICK shrugs.

                          RICK
Seemed like the best thing to do at the time. We were beef-
ing a lot, my dad and me. Teenage stuff. You know. I had quit
school and he didn't like that. So I left.

GLORIA

Why'd you quit?

RICK

I hated it? I don't know. I was stupid back then.

GLORIA

What did you do after you left?

RICK

Worked. Whatever I could pick up. Paper route. Bag boy. Nonunion construction. Pizza delivery. Whatever.

GLORIA

What did you want to be at this point? Did you have any career aspirations?

A moment.

RICK

"Career aspirations?" I think that's a bit more than I was capable of back then.
   (*Shyly*)
I had—some ideas, I guess, of maybe being, like, an architect.

GLORIA

Why?

RICK

I liked—building things. The idea of building things. Things that last.

GLORIA

You never studied?

RICK

Got some brochures from a junior college but—

GLORIA

And then you joined the Army?

RICK

Had to get my GED first but that was no real problem.

GLORIA

Tested out on your first try. Impressive.

RICK

Turns out I'm not stupid. In fact, my IQ is—something. Pretty high, I was told.

GLORIA

Why did you join up?

RICK

We were at war.

                    GLORIA

9/11.

                    RICK

Yeah.

                    GLORIA

Patriotic.

                    RICK

What's wrong with that?

                    GLORIA

Nothing. My brother joined up.

                    RICK

Army?

                    GLORIA

Marines.

                    RICK

Marines. Wow. He still in?

                    GLORIA

He died over there.

    A moment.

RICK

I'm sorry.

GLORIA

Me, too. He was my favorite brother. I didn't want him to go but he thought he should. Like you, he saw it as a duty. We argued about it a lot.

RICK

What happened?
  (*Quickly*)
You don't have to tell me.

A moment.

GLORIA

I don't mind. Now. I did at first. At first, I couldn't talk to anybody, I just, I just shut down. Grief, yes. Of course. But I was so angry. I think I held on to that because my anger was all I had left that connected him to me. And I drank to, to numb everything else. I had a dream about him. Once. Woke up and he was sitting beside me on the bed. No big message from the Beyond. He just sat there and looked at me. And he, uh, he held my hand. And I woke up. Eventually it became clear to me that both the anger and the alcohol were holding me back and so I started to let go of both of them. And after a while I could talk about him. I think it's good to talk about what weighs on your heart. It was for me, anyway. It didn't change the facts any but I felt better. Eventually. Three weeks into his tour, his Humvee hit an IED. I was told he died instantly.

(*Beat*)

It was a closed casket service.

RICK

I really wanted to be a Marine but—there was just no way.

(*Embarrassed*)

Flat feet.

GLORIA

Trump got out of service in Vietnam claiming he had bone spurs.

RICK

I wasn't trying to get out of service, I wanted in! There's a difference.

GLORIA

Right. Sorry.

RICK

And what difference does it make? Bush ducked service in Vietnam and so did your precious Bill Clinton. It was a different war.

GLORIA

Good point. You don't have a problem with people like them
touting patriotism while avoiding service?

RICK

Hey, all politicians lie. It's part of the game.

GLORIA

So how do we judge which politician is good and who isn't?

RICK

By what they do.

GLORIA

So we should judge people not by their rhetoric and not by
their intentions but by their actions?

*A moment. RICK looks uncomfortable. In the distance, some-
body screams. Both GLORIA and RICK glance toward the
door.*

GLORIA

Is there a lot of that?

RICK shrugs.

RICK

Define a lot.

GLORIA

So you went Army. Did you have a choice in area of service?

RICK

In theory. I mean, I told them I wanted to serve in a combat unit.

GLORIA

But that didn't work out.

RICK

They made promises sure, but no, it didn't. I mean I was in a combat *zone*, so I guess, technically, I was.

GLORIA

How did you wind up in military police?

RICK

It was so stupid! They ask you for your work experience, right? And the last job I had was a part-time night watchman for a H-E-B food store.

GLORIA
(*Smiling*)
You said you worked "security."

RICK

I didn't lie exactly. I just described it as, maybe a little more than it was.

GLORIA

What did you think of being an MP?

RICK

After I got over bein' pissed about it I kinda liked it.

GLORIA

Why?

RICK

I liked—I liked the order, the organization of the Army a lot, even when it was messed up, it had a, a structure, you know. Clean lines of authority. I liked being part of what maintained that structure. I liked bringing order.

GLORIA

You were very good at it, too, apparently. Lot of positive comments in your jacket.

RICK

That surprise you?

GLORIA

I wasn't passing judgment; just offering an observation.

RICK

OK. Yeah, so, that was part of it. I was good at something for once. Really good. And it wasn't that hard. If you did your job like you were supposed to do, when you were supposed to do it, you moved up. I liked that a lot. It was clear.

GLORIA

Multiple promotions during your four years of active duty resulting in your being a sergeant when you left. Where did you serve?

RICK

Stateside: Fort Riley and Fort Hood. Overseas: Kuwait, Saudi Arabia, Iraq.

GLORIA

What was that like?

RICK

I liked Fort Hood, made some good friends there. One of them was killed in that shooting.

GLORIA

Nidal Hasan in 2009?

RICK

Yeah. My buddy, John Reich, he stayed in the service, toured all over the place, including a lot of really dangerous assignments, and then he comes back to Fort Hood and gets killed as he's walking into the PX. Left a wife and two young kids behind. That got me thinking about the whole illegal immigrant thing.

A moment.

GLORIA

Nidal wasn't an immigrant. He was born here.

RICK

Yeah, well, his parents were immigrants.

GLORIA

So, how far back should we go in terms of immigration policy? To be safe. One generation? Two? How does that work? I mean, at some point in the past we were all immigrants, right, except for Native Americans.

RICK

What about those guys on 9/11?

GLORIA

None of them were immigrants. They were all on visas.

RICK

The Boston guys were immigrants.

GLORIA

They came with their parents as kids but none of them were illegal. In fact, the second most devastating terrorist attack in the history of the United States, the Oklahoma bombing, was carried out by a US citizen, born and raised. And white. And Christian.

RICK

A country has a right to protect its borders! If we don't have borders, then we don't have a country. What's so hard about understanding that?

GLORIA

I wouldn't disagree that borders need protecting, the question I guess is from whom and how?
(*Beat*)
What was your experience of the Middle East?

RICK

What I remember most is hot and I don't mean that in a good way. Hot as in fry an egg on your forehead. And boring. Claustrophobic. You could never really leave the base and go into town. Made people antsy. We had a lot of trouble with discipline, drinking, drugs, stupid shit.

GLORIA

I've seen your service report but for the record, did you serve at Abu Ghraib?

RICK

No. Contrary to the fake news out there, I did not.

GLORIA

Did you know some of the people who did serve there?

RICK

Sure.

GLORIA

What were your feelings about that?

A moment.

RICK

Whatever I say is going to be misunderstood. Or used against me.

GLORIA

I think you're probably right but then you're also in a unique position to comment; few people have your experience.

RICK

(*Drily*)

Or would want it.

(*Beat*)

OK. You had a situation that got out of control, obviously. Why? Chaotic conditions resulted from a lack of infrastructure, absurd overcrowding, inadequate training, poor discipline, and confusion over mission goals.

GLORIA

You subscribe to the "few bad apples" theory?

RICK

I think that's a very convenient way for the Brass to cover their ass. Rumsfeld certainly seems to be doing all right now, don't you think? Big book sale and all. And what was the top officer convicted in any of that? Lieutenant Colonel Jordan. And then six months later he's cleared of all wrongdoing. They tossed a lotta little people into the trash and then congratulated themselves.

GLORIA

Karpinski was demoted.

RICK

Sure. Dereliction of duty and *shoplifting*. Jesus wept.

GLORIA

Defense Contractor Engility Holdings paid over five million dollars to former detainees.

RICK

Wow. That must of hurt. You know what they earned that year? 3.7 billion dollars.

GLORIA

You left the Army in 2005. Why?

RICK

I joined up 'cause of 9/11 and after Saddam was captured I felt like, I don't know, "Mission Accomplished."

GLORIA

Iraq of course had nothing to do with 9/11.

RICK

(*Grim humor*)
Well, we weren't going to invade Saudi Arabia, were we?

GLORIA

(*Nodding*)
Where most of the 9/11 hijackers were from. Weirdly, Trump also excluded Saudi Arabia from his first Muslim travel ban.

RICK

That's all above my pay grade. My term was up and you could feel a troop reduction was coming one way or another and I just didn't see a future for myself in the Army. And I had met Stacey by then and being overseas didn't have much appeal any more.

GLORIA

How'd you meet your wife? Soon to be wife.

RICK

I don't want to talk about her. We're not going to talk about my wife in here. She had nothing to do with any of this.

A moment.

GLORIA

OK. So, you went home and joined law enforcement. Why?

RICK

(*Grins*)

Well, Harvard Law School turned me down. It's what I knew. All I knew. Why not?

GLORIA

You worked a number of years in various state law enforcement agencies and then finally joined the private sector in 2008.

RICK

Yes, GEO.

GLORIA

Why them?

RICK

It's where the money was.

GLORIA

And you wound up working in Pecos, Texas, at the Reeves County Detention Complex, which is the largest private prison in the world. Or it was.

RICK

We were under contract with the Federal Bureau of Prisons and the Arizona Department of Corrections.

GLORIA

How many inmates?

RICK

When I was there, close to four thousand.

GLORIA

Who were the inmates?

RICK

Criminal aliens. Drug offenses or immigration violations. Usually serving one to five. Most get deported on release.

GLORIA

Did you enjoy your work?

RICK

(*Shrugs*)
It was OK.

GLORIA

What were your feelings about the facility?

RICK

We had two security situations in my first fourteen months.
After that, things calmed down.

GLORIA

Security situations. You mean riots?

RICK

I wouldn't call it that. It wasn't that serious.

GLORIA

Why was there a problem?

RICK

Usual stuff.

GLORIA glances at her notes.

GLORIA

There were claims of substandard medical care.

RICK

Yes.

GLORIA

Given what would later happen in El Paso, that kind of
jumps out at you.

RICK

Apples and oranges.

GLORIA

So you wouldn't describe the medical care as substandard.

RICK

Prisons are not generally thought of as a place that's supposed to be "comfortable." People don't want criminals to be comfortable, they want them to be punished. And a "for-profit" facility has additional pressures to keep an eye on the bottom line. So, I would say the medical care was definitely not lavish but I wouldn't describe it as substandard.

GLORIA

In a seven-month period there, five men died, including an epileptic Mexican citizen, Jesus Manuel Galindo, who was denied medical treatment despite repeated pleas for help.

RICK

"A Mexican citizen." Some people would say that if Mr. Galindo hadn't been illegally in the United States in the first place that none of that would have happened.

GLORIA

Are you one of those people?
(*No response*)
Do you think Mr. Galindo deserved to die?

RICK

If you will note, a year after my arrival medical services improved and there were no more riots. I'm very proud of that.

GLORIA

Are you suggesting one led to the other? Because I also see that during your management security forces were substantially increased, as was the use of long-term isolation units. In May 2013 *Mother Jones* magazine called it "one of the ten worst prisons in the United States."

RICK

Mother Jones magazine. There's a, what do you call it, a very objective news source. Come on.

GLORIA

In August 2016 the Justice Department publicly announced they would be phasing out the use of all contracted facilities—private prisons.

RICK

But they didn't, did they?

GLORIA

No, the election changed that. On February 23, 2017, then–Attorney General Jeff Sessions announced that he was in support of private prisons. Stock prices of major private prisons rose immediately. For the record, private prison corporations had given generously to the Trump campaign. I'm sure that's just a coincidence.

RICK

Kinda the name of the game, isn't it? On both sides? Pay to play.

GLORIA

Would you describe yourself as political at that time?

RICK

Not really. No.

GLORIA

Party affiliation?

RICK

Republican.

GLORIA

Why?

RICK

I don't know. My dad was. They're tougher on crime, I guess. I like lower taxes. The first president I voted for was Bush. The younger.

GLORIA

Was he a good president?

RICK

He kicked bin Laden's ass.

GLORIA

But bin Laden survived. It was under President Obama that bin Laden was finally killed. And Bush invaded Iraq under false pretenses.

RICK

And Obama invaded Libya.

GLORIA

We never invaded Libya.

RICK

Maybe we should have.

GLORIA

Because Iraq worked out so well?

RICK

Look, Bush, Obama, two sides of the same coin far as I'm concerned. Neither of them really cared about people like me. Or you.

GLORIA

What do you mean?

RICK

Working people. Middle class. Everybody talked about how well the country was doing but not my people. I had friends losing their houses, their jobs. My dad had some health problems and it turns out, his insurance didn't cover much of anything and it ate up his retirement and within a year, suddenly he was working as a greeter at Walmart! Seventy-something years old, standing on his feet eight hours a day working for less than minimum. Meanwhile all our jobs were going to Mexico and China and places like that and then the illegals here taking what jobs are left and nobody gave a damn. For a long time I wasn't paying attention but then I woke up pretty fast because it was clear the country was going into the toilet.

GLORIA

Were you a Trump supporter from the beginning?

RICK

Not at first. I never claimed to be one of "The Originals."

GLORIA

But your record shows otherwise.

A moment.

RICK

That's one of the things I wanted to explain. I had a friend, see, really a friend of a friend, who said at the time that he could get my name into the records as an "Original" and it wouldn't cost me all that much and that it would be helpful down the line, you know, professionally, a good connection, so I said sure and I never really thought much about it after that but that was all after the election. Before, before the election, during the primaries, I didn't know what to make of him. I mean, I knew he was a gazillionaire. Had his name all over everything. Trump this and Trump that. He was on that TV show where he fired people but one night I was in a bar with some friends and one of those early debates was on TV and he was very entertaining, you know? The way he would put down those stuffed shirts and leave them standing there in a little flop-sweat pool of their canned bullshit. It was funny. You could see the gears in their machinery grind to a halt 'cause they didn't know what to do with him. And the nicknames! Little Rubio. Low Energy Bush. Lying Ted. He just zinged 'em. They were like a lotta fish you pulled outta the water and threw up on the bank and there they are, gasping for air, all goggle-eyed. It was funny. And it felt good to see these guys who just, like Jeb Bush, you know, he just seemed to think he was "owed" the presidency because of his name, his family, and there he was, Trump making fun of him on TV and Bush looking all pained like he suddenly had a bad case of hemorrhoids or something.

GLORIA

So you got into him, Trump.

RICK

I went to a rally. I don't really know why, I guess I just thought it would be fun, you know, and I was kinda curious. So, he did a rally in Dallas on my day off—

GLORIA

You've switched companies now, you're working for a new private prison company, Magnum Security—

RICK

Yeah, Magnum.

GLORIA

Why?

RICK

'Cause they offered me a raise and more responsibility overseeing their new facility outside of El Paso. So I went to the rally and it was amazing. I felt—I felt—*comfortable* there.

GLORIA

Comfortable. Why?

RICK

I looked around and I saw a lotta people who looked like me, just ordinary people, people with families.

GLORIA

White. White people.

RICK

Yeah. I guess. Mostly. Sure.

GLORIA

Christian.

RICK

What's wrong with that?

GLORIA

Nothing.

RICK

No, the way you ask that, it seems like there is and I wonder about that, I got to wondering about that at that rally, I mean if you can have Gay Pride and Black Pride and Trans-Whatever Pride, why can't I be proud to be white?

Why can't I be proud to be Christian? Who speaks up for us anymore? And it seemed like he did. Trump would say these things, kind of edgy, you know, things you're not "supposed to say" and he would say them and you could feel the crowd, you could feel the crowd kind of jump because a line had been crossed, or a line that you had been told all your life you couldn't cross and now here it had been crossed in public and lightning hadn't come down and struck this guy, in fact, he looked really happy, and then you could feel the crowd relax, like this enormous weight had been taken off their shoulders, and then there would be this little electric thrill like, I don't know, like when you were a kid and you did something you had been told was wrong but you did it anyway. That little jolt. And then the crowd would get really lively. They would start shouting back at him. And that would work him up. And back and forth. It was like being part of a wave or something. Big. Bigger than yourself. You didn't feel little anymore, you didn't feel put down anymore. Shamed. You didn't feel *shamed* anymore.

GLORIA

What about the violence at his rallies? Saying Hillary should be locked up or "taken care of by those Second Amendment people." Asking the crowd whether non-Christians should be allowed to stay. Keeping out, even arresting certain reporters. Protestors getting beaten up.

RICK

Hey, those guys were there to provoke people and they succeeded. I mean the whole thing was all a kind of, kind of, I don't
know, like pro-wrestling thing, you know? A performance.

GLORIA

Some people got really hurt.

RICK

Nobody died.

GLORIA

No, that would be later.

A moment.

GLORIA

So you got involved. Politically.

RICK

Small things at first. Help put up yard signs, hand out fliers,
work the phones.

GLORIA

And then you started doing security.

RICK

I handled security for two events in Texas, that's all.

GLORIA

And that's where you met him, met Trump.

RICK

Yeah.

GLORIA

What was that like?

A moment.

RICK

I was onstage before the rally, checking security, when he came out with his bodyguard to check the on-set lighting. He does that *himself.* He pays that kind of attention to detail. You know. Think about it. So, anyway I just kept doing my thing, you know, and his bodyguard came over and said Mr. Trump would like to meet you and I walked over and he nodded at me, asked me my name, and told me I was doing a good job.

GLORIA

That was it.

RICK

That was pretty cool! I mean, I wasn't anybody special and he took the time to say hello.

A moment.

GLORIA

I have to ask. The hands. Are they small?

RICK laughs. Leans in, confidingly.

RICK

They kinda are.

GLORIA laughs.

GLORIA

Did he shake your hand?

RICK

Are you kidding? He doesn't do that. Too many germs. That's how he stays so healthy. He didn't get pneumonia and faint.

GLORIA

Like Hillary.

RICK

Yeah.

GLORIA

What turned you off about her?

RICK

What doesn't? She's a liar. Benghazi. The email thing. The
foundation.

GLORIA

Oh, come on. Most of that was blown completely out of pro-
portion and there's no comparison with Trump. Every time
he opened his mouth, he lied.

RICK

I don't see it that way.
    (*Beat*)
I mean, OK, yeah, he lied, but all politicians lie, right? I get
that. So part of that was him doing what he had to do but
he was also telling a lot of hard truth, too. Knocking *both*
parties, not just Democrats, for their bullshit about NAFTA,
and Iraq, and NATO.

GLORIA

And immigrants.

A moment.

RICK

Sure. Yeah. That was a big part of it.

GLORIA

So, what's your take on that?

RICK

I'm not—nobody believes this of course and I get that, I understand that after, after everything, but I'm not prejudiced like people think. I don't care who you are or where you're from but people shouldn't be able to come into this country illegally and take away our jobs and use our services and resources, that just seems pretty clear to me. And of course I'm not alone in this. He won the election.

GLORIA

He won the electoral college. Hillary beat him by over three million in the popular vote.

RICK

He *won*. That's the rules of the game. You don't get to whine about it after.

GLORIA

You think if it had been reversed, her winning the electoral vote and him winning the popular vote, he would have accepted it?

RICK

Well, we'll never know, will we?

A moment.

GLORIA

You think when people voted for him they were voting for the imposition of martial law?

RICK

People were voting to get their country back!
   (*Beat*)
And then after the Times Square thing people were pissed.
It was 9/11 all over again.

GLORIA

A lot of people now wonder if the Times Square event wasn't
a kind of false flag operation.

RICK

A fake attack? People died. Two square blocks *irradiated*.

GLORIA

Not that the attack didn't happen—of course it did—what
is being questioned is the narrative: *who* set it off? And why?

RICK

Why is it when conservatives wonder about stuff like
this, conspiracies, we're being paranoid but when liberals
do, they're being smart? Maybe it's not all that complicated. A Muslim terrorist tried to blow up two bombs
in New York just a few months earlier when Obama was
still president and we were just lucky the second bomb
didn't go off.

GLORIA

Because two other Muslim men disarmed the second
bomb.

RICK

By accident! "Dumpster-diving heroes." The point is, this time we didn't get lucky. We got hit. And people finally started to get what Trump had been talking about, about the illegals and how dangerous they are.

GLORIA

The men arrested for the bombing didn't enter the country illegally. They were born here.

RICK

They were Muslim. And the truck they used *was* owned by an illegal immigrant. From *Mexico*.

GLORIA

Mr. Ortiz is Catholic. So, the conspiracy here is between Muslims and Catholics? How does that work?

RICK

He *claims* he's Catholic; how do we know?

GLORIA

Mr. Ortiz says his truck was stolen.

RICK

Why didn't he report it then?

GLORIA

Probably because he didn't have papers and figured the

loss of the truck was better than being deported. Or worse.

A moment.

RICK

This is what I don't get about liberals. Look, like it or not, we're in a war. That was Trump's point. Like it or not, it's a fact that ISIS declared war on us; radical Islam has declared war on us. People like you tie yourself in knots trying to explain things away but usually the simplest explanation is the truth.

GLORIA

I think people like to believe that, people like to believe that problems are simple and solutions are simple but I don't think that's the case. There's a "simple" explanation for what you did but you reject that, or your lawyer did at your trial. He claimed all kinds of mitigating circumstances, all kinds of theories, in your defense.

RICK
(*Quietly*)
We can argue all you want about Times Square but the point is, it happened, and people turned to the president to take charge.

GLORIA

So he declares martial law and starts rounding people up.

RICK

He protects Americans, real Americans, and starts fulfilling his campaign promise to deport illegals. Not exactly a surprise since he'd been talking about that since the beginning. And come on, we've been "rounding people up" forever. Eisenhower was doing it in the fifties in "Operation Wetback." Even your precious liberal Obama, he kicked out way more illegals than Bush ever did!

GLORIA

In his first four years, yes, then deportations—

RICK

Removals.

GLORIA

Sorry?

RICK

Since we're being all precise here, the Department of Homeland Security calls them "removals."

GLORIA

OK, removals, but in the last four years of the Obama administration that number had been cut in half.

RICK

But it was happening! Been happening. As American as

apple pie. All countries have the right to protect their borders.

GLORIA

Within the rule of law.

RICK

Martial law is law.

GLORIA

It doesn't permit anything and everything. If it did, you wouldn't be sitting here, would you?

RICK

I'm sitting here because that's what always happens. Shit rolls downhill and the little guy takes the fall while the people who really set things in motion, they always walk. Always.

GLORIA

Trump isn't walking.

RICK

Impeached. Exiled to Palm Beach. Wow. That must sting.

A moment.

GLORIA

So, let's talk about how you did wind up here.
(*Beat*)

Trump wins. Doesn't waste any time and on January 31st, issues his first executive order curtailing immigration. Chaos results.

RICK

They kinda screwed the pooch on that one.

GLORIA

Nine days later the courts block the administration. They regroup. On February 22nd, Homeland Security issues two memos that basically eliminate most of the restrictions for removal, and now immigration officials—or local police officers or sheriffs—can arrest anybody *they think could be a risk to public safety or national security.* Some states respond by passing laws forbidding local police forces to serve as de facto immigration officers and then the Times Square event happens. The president declares martial law and the roundup begins.

RICK

The roundup *continues*. The system had been in place forever and we'd been arresting and removing people for years, we'd just never done it in these kinds of numbers before.

GLORIA

Millions.

RICK

Over eleven million people. That's what we thought anyway because, of course, there's no way to know for sure.

GLORIA

It's complicated.

RICK

Hell, yeah! You got people who came over illegally but then they had children here. So, legally, the kids are legal while the parents are not. What do you do? Throw the parents over the border but allow the two-year-old to stay? How does that work? So Congress fixed that.

GLORIA

The "Comprehensive Reform Immigration and Expulsion Act of 2017."

RICK

Right. They passed a law. That's their job.

GLORIA

Senate Republicans discard the filibuster rule and despite massive public demonstrations around the country push it through.

RICK

But *legal.* Everything they did was legal.

GLORIA

Did any of this bother you? That now, for instance, your parents had to have been in this country legally in order for you to be legal and *you had to be able to prove that* and if you can't, then everybody has to go.

RICK
Well, if you were a kid, that sucks, sure, but why should somebody, anybody, benefit from a criminal act? If somebody robs a bank and drops a bag of money, can I pick it up and claim it, just because I didn't hold up the bank? What do they call that, "fruit of the poisoned tree," right?

GLORIA
It seems almost certain now, that the Supreme Court will overturn it.

RICK
Maybe, but for those of us on the ground *at the time* we were tasked with what was clearly the intent of Congress.

A moment.

GLORIA
So the roundups begin but the numbers are huge.

RICK shakes his head.

RICK
The whole thing was a clusterfuck of massive proportions.

GLORIA

What were the problems, from your viewpoint, I mean, on the ground?

RICK

OK. So, you're arresting all these people and some of them have just arrived and some of them have been in the country for years, decades maybe, and some of them are clearly illegal and some weren't illegal before but now they are illegal and however you wanna slice it, there are a helluva lot of people. Where do you put 'em? All our normal facilities were completely overwhelmed.

GLORIA

What do we mean by normal?

RICK

OK, so before this whole thing blew up, about 30 percent of illegal detainees were in facilities owned by state and local governments, and 20 percent were in space contracted with the US Marshals Service. And then some state and local facilities subcontracted with for-profit prison companies.

GLORIA

Which is where you come in.

RICK

Right. So, suddenly, there's this big push to arrest and detain but not only are the numbers insane but the program to deport hits a snag—

GLORIA

—when Mexico and twenty-three other countries refuse to accept.

RICK

Refuse to accept their own citizens! That's kind of fucked up.

GLORIA

Why should they? Some of them like Mexico saw it as refusing to participate, and by participating, appear to endorse what they considered a racist, immoral, and illegal system. The same reason a number of American counties and even states took issue with the new policy.

RICK

Or maybe they just didn't want those people either. Whatever the reason, the arrests are happening and people are stacking up. Normal facilities are overwhelmed. So, the government turns to the private sector because we can move faster.

GLORIA

So you're now working for Magnum Security—

RICK

At this new facility miles outside El Paso near an industrial park.

GLORIA

Why there?

RICK

Typically, private prisons are sited in somewhat remote areas. Security reasons.

GLORIA

(*Drily*)
Avoidance of burdensome local regulations?

RICK

I guess. Sure. All corporations build where their costs are cheapest, so why should private prisons be any different?

GLORIA

What was the facility like?

RICK

It was really good. At first. I mean, they'd learned a lot of lessons by now and they built new and converted some existing buildings into a pretty solid complex. We had three housing facilities, a medical clinic, kitchen.

GLORIA

Did you advise them at all? I mean with your practical experience and your architectural interests that would make sense.

RICK

(*Cautiously*)
When they asked my opinion, I gave it. How to make things flow better. Security. Etcetera.

GLORIA

What was security like?

RICK

Standard. Double barbed-wire fences eight feet apart with armed guards.

GLORIA

That's standard?

RICK

Pretty much.

GLORIA

So you're there. How did things work?

RICK

Pretty much like they always had. At first. We would get groups of deportees usually in buses or vans.

GLORIA

Handcuffed?

RICK

And sometimes shackled. Hey, some of these people were felons, convicted of serious crimes, violent crimes.

GLORIA

Did you separate the felons out from the other people, the illegal aliens?

RICK

At first, yes, later that became impossible and I didn't like it. I raised a stink about it but I never got any help. So, we would process the paperwork and get them squared away.

GLORIA

What does that entail, "squaring away?"

RICK

All personal possessions are removed and catalogued. Every detainee is issued an orange jumpsuit.
RICK gestures wryly at his own uniform.
Like this fetching number. And you get issued a bed and the number of that bed or your registration number then becomes your ID.

GLORIA

No names.

RICK

It's easier that way. I mean you get a lot of "Jones" or "Juans" or "Muhammads" or whatever, it's too confusing.

GLORIA

What do people do when they're there?

RICK

Wait.

GLORIA

That's it?

RICK

Well, I mean, there are head counts three to four times a day and you're always required to be standing by your bed when a count is going on. You're allowed visitors on a very limited basis. Your lawyer, whatever. Very few phones, so if you want to use the phone you have to put your name on a list and wait.

GLORIA

No books? No TV?

RICK

There are a few TVs in the communal areas. Books, yeah, I guess. Bibles were permitted.

GLORIA

The Koran?

RICK

Sure. See, we're not a prison, really, well we are and we aren't, what I mean is, people aren't expected to stay here, so there's no rehabilitation thing going on, we're just supposed to hold them and then process them out.

GLORIA

Do families stay together?

RICK

I'm a big believer in that because it calms people down, reduces a lot of anxiety.

GLORIA

Efficient.

RICK

(*Sharply*)
I just think it's the right thing to do.

A moment. GLORIA nods. Takes a note.

RICK

Anyway, that's the way we started but it became harder and harder when the numbers started to ramp up.

GLORIA

Can you give me an example?

RICK

So, usually, in normal times, you're getting, I don't know, maybe twenty to forty people a day and then you're processing out about the same, sometimes a little more, sometimes a little less.

GLORIA

Process out?

RICK

Repatriate.

GLORIA

Bus?
   (*Slightest pause*)
Plane?

RICK

All of the above, depending on where they're from but when the Expulsion Act was ratified the numbers started to ratchet up so fast and everybody was overwhelmed. I mean, they were arresting people right and left and dumping them in whatever prisons that would take them.

GLORIA
And not all prisons would take them.

RICK
(*Nodding*)
The Feds didn't have that much room to begin with and most states were already crowded and some got to feeling a little hinky about the whole thing and so it pretty much came down to the private sector, to people like us. So, suddenly a ton of inflow. At the same time, Mexico and other countries started refusing repatriation, so here we are trying to kick them out but nobody would take them so you got this terrible overflow that's just getting worse every day and these people in limbo.

GLORIA
Sounds crazy.

RICK
It was fucking nuts! We doubled and tripled up everywhere we could but pretty quickly that wasn't going to work. Security was a nightmare. So, we kind of borrowed a page from Sheriff Arpaio and put up some tent facilities in the exercise yard, mostly for the single men, but I didn't like that.

GLORIA

Why?

RICK

From a security and organizational standpoint it's not ideal and conditions are extremely uncomfortable.

GLORIA

Comfort was a concern of yours?

RICK

I'm not some freaking sadist, all right! I was doing the absolute best I could for everybody, working around the clock, pulling every string I had.

A moment.

GLORIA

I'm just trying to understand, Rick, given what happened—

RICK

I'm just a guy, all right, a regular guy in extraordinary circumstances trying to do the best he can with very limited resources—

GLORIA

You're in charge of the facility—

RICK

I'm one in a long chain of responsibility with a lot of people to answer to. To the extent I could, I did the best I could to, to, to mitigate things. And when everything, when things turned serious, you know, it wasn't like I jumped at the opportunity. Oh boy! This is gonna be fun! It was never like that. Never.

GLORIA

Why didn't you quit?

A moment. RICK shakes his head.

RICK

Because it was my shop and my people, and some of those guys I had worked with for years and they'd followed me there, and I was just, what, going to abandon them? No way. Maybe it's old-fashioned but loyalty counts for something in my book. And it's a two-way street. And who would replace me? I mean, it probably would've been a lot worse.

GLORIA

Worse than what happened?
(*No response*)
Was it your idea to use the football stadium?

RICK

Yes.

GLORIA

Why?

RICK

It had obvious advantages.

GLORIA

Such as?

RICK

Nearby. Had a lot of bathrooms. Facilities to cook and distribute food. Some shelter from the elements. Quantifiable egress and entrance gates, so it was easier from a security point of view.

GLORIA

How did the detainees react to the stadium?

RICK

I think initially it was seen as an improvement, especially if you were in the tent city in the yard, but some people, it made them anxious.

GLORIA

Why?
  (*Beat*)
Why did it make them anxious, Rick?

RICK

I didn't know this at the time, all right, I'm no historian, but in some countries apparently, some South American countries, stadiums had been used as detention centers by governments and a lot of bad things happened there.

GLORIA

Argentina. Chile. Mexico.

RICK

I honestly think we would have been fine except for the sanitation problem.

GLORIA

Cholera.

RICK

That many people all crowded together, the issue is always sanitation, disposal of human waste. Initially the stadium was working OK but the people just kept coming and I had done everything I could, bringing in as many honey wagons as I could find but demand was exceeding supply and it was harder and harder to get them maintained properly. The corporation was just not responding on this issue and I was always being told to make do. I brought in industrial-sized containers of hand sanitizer and I trucked in water for drinking and cleaning but you're just rolling the dice in a situation like that and eventually it caught up with us. The first case of cholera was in August, August 22nd. It was hot as hell, so we were already experiencing dehydration in kids, in the elderly, in immune-compromised individuals.

GLORIA

And these people were in the general population, you hadn't been able to maintain separate populations, right?

RICK

Not after the population boom, no, it just got crazy, more and more people arriving every day. I would be on the phone asking for help, asking for more resources, telling them we were full up and the answer was always the same.

GLORIA

What?

RICK

"Figure it out."

GLORIA

So, August, middle of a heat wave, and people start getting sick.

RICK

Cholera. You ever have any experience with that? It's devastating. Violent diarrhea. Vomiting and muscle cramps. As soon as we figured out what we were dealing with we did the usual things, rehydration combined with antibiotics but the thing with cholera is it's just so fucking fast, we had the first fatalities within two hours. It was just, just terrifying. All our initial stocks of oral rehydration were gone in half a day and forget IV use. We were making our own makeshift compound out of table salt and sugar but we didn't have any potassium supplements and pretty soon we were having to triage the situation.

GLORIA
"Triage the situation?"

A moment.

GLORIA
What do you mean, triage the situation?

RICK
(*Quietly*)
Decide who got medicine and who didn't.

GLORIA
And if they didn't?

RICK
Then, the odds weren't great for them.

GLORIA

They were more likely to die.

RICK

(*Irritated*)

Yes.

GLORIA

How did you decide?

RICK

It wasn't just me deciding. I wasn't the "Decider in Chief."
Actually, it wasn't me at all, you know, going bedside to bedside or whatever.

GLORIA

Medical staff?

RICK

We were understaffed, as I said, so yeah, medical staff
at first and then you had guards, prison guards with
no training for this kinda situation having to make
choices.

GLORIA

There are stories of guards selling rehydration meds to the
highest bidders.

RICK

I only heard of one case like that and I fired his ass immediately!

GLORIA

So it happened.

RICK

Not like some people suggest but yes, of course it happened!
It's human nature. People were desperate, their family members were dying, their kids, their spouses, their siblings were
dying and if you got the medicine then you probably lived
so you did what you had to do. Wouldn't you? And there's
always somebody who will take advantage of that.

GLORIA

What did they trade with? I thought when people came into
detention they lost all their private goods.

RICK

Initially, yes, but when we got overwhelmed my people got
sloppy. So there was anything you could smuggle in: money,
jewelry, drugs, the usual stuff in prisons.

GLORIA

And if you didn't have any of those things?

RICK

I suppose you, you bartered. Traded.

GLORIA

With what?
   (*Beat*)
Sex?

RICK

Yes. Probably some people did.

GLORIA

So, people were offering sex to save family members.

RICK

Later I heard that.

GLORIA

You didn't know that at the time.

RICK

I had an infectious outbreak on my hands, I wasn't paying close attention to who was fucking who!

A moment.

GLORIA

What was the attitude of the staff to all of this?

RICK

My people tried to be professional about it but like I said, we were overwhelmed and some people were freaked out. These are guards not nurses. Cholera is—the smell alone is— It was hard to hang on to your compassion and a lot of people were scared and, and angry, I guess.

GLORIA

Angry?

RICK

Yeah, you know, the whole thing about illegals being rapists and murderers, being unclean and bringing disease into the country and here they were so sick and all and some guys felt, well, they felt like they brought this on themselves. And you gotta remember, my people were exhausted, they were pulling double and triple shifts and the situation was just chaotic and every problem seemed to lead to another problem so you never could get a moment to catch your breath and think things through.

GLORIA

What other problems?

A moment.

RICK

Bodies. Suddenly we had these bodies piling up and our mortuary just wasn't equipped to handle the volume and the heat made the situation even worse. I called corporate and they were supposed to get me some portable mortuaries like FEMA used in Katrina but they were so slow in coming and they told me to call the city and the county and I did that, and I even called the state but nobody wanted any part of it, you know, everybody just kicked the can down the road. You deal with it.

GLORIA

So people knew what was going on?

RICK

People always knew! Look, the location was somewhat remote but we had guys coming and going all the time, making deliveries. And then the staff goes home at night and people talk, you know, they talk to their spouses, their neighbors. This idea that we were out there doing terrible things and NOBODY knew is bullshit! At the trial, you never saw so many goddamn virgins all of sudden.

GLORIA

When you went home at night did you talk to Stacey?

RICK

No.

GLORIA

Why?

RICK

(*Struggling*)
I wanted to keep her out of it. All right. It just felt like, like

the one place in my life that wasn't—if I could keep that separate, I could just—

(*Beat*)

Eventually, I went home less and less. It was just easier. I had a cot put up in my office and slept there. When I slept.

GLORIA

So you had a problem with bodies.

RICK

We had a problem. So while I was waiting for somebody to throw me a rope I tried to make some kind of makeshift thing but I was worried we were going to lose control of the whole situation from a health standpoint.

GLORIA

At this point you had your first visit from corporate.
    (*Checking her notes*)
Richards.

RICK

Yes, a vice president of operations named Jack Richards.

GLORIA

Your lawyer talked about him a lot at your trial but of course, nothing could be substantiated because Richards was dead by then.

RICK

Hung himself awaiting trial. They say.

GLORIA

You don't believe that?

RICK

With a trash bag?

GLORIA

Interesting you don't believe that. That's what they said about Sandra Bland. That she hung herself with a trash bag. A lot of people, a lot of black people, don't believe that either.

RICK

I don't know anything about that.

GLORIA

You're inclined to believe a conspiracy in the former but not in the latter?

RICK

Kinda off-topic aren't we?

A moment.

GLORIA

So you finally had the attention of corporate headquarters and Jack Richards shows up. What was that like?

RICK

At first I was so grateful because, you know, I had a real crisis on my hands but Richards didn't seem to care about any of that except in so much as how it might look, the publicity angle and shit. They were making money hand over fist at this point—

GLORIA

The so-called "Trump roundup" was in full force. Deportation squads in all major cities plus those people, the paramilitaries who were self-deputizing themselves in order to participate. Citizen's arrest.

RICK

Again, I'm not dealing with any of that, just the result. And I wasn't getting much help from Richards because there looked like a lot more Fed contracts would be let and we were likely to get a big share of those too, so mostly Richards just wanted the problem to go away.

GLORIA

Go away?

RICK

We had dinner at TGI Fridays and he talked about it in very clinical terms. "A sanitation problem." Troublesome, potentially embarrassing "disposal issues." Emergency situation requiring out of the box thinking.

GLORIA

So what happened?

A moment.

RICK

So we, we started, you know—

A moment.

GLORIA

Burning the bodies.

RICK

Yeah.

GLORIA

Where?

RICK

We did an experiment first. There was a landfill-garbage dump five miles away and we first started trucking bodies there but—but even with an accelerant like diesel fuel, it's harder than you might think.

GLORIA

Who was participating in these experiments? These were guards?

RICK

Guards. At first. And then some detainees.

GLORIA

Detainees?

RICK

We were short-staffed. So, we recruited people.

GLORIA

Recruited how?

RICK

With privileges. Medicine. Extra food.

GLORIA

They didn't protest?

RICK

(*Dryly*)

I imagine they were pretty intimidated.

GLORIA

So, the landfill option didn't work very well.

RICK

Inefficient like I said but also we were getting complaints about the smoke, the smell, I mean it was insane. Everybody had a problem with what we were doing but nobody was offering any solutions and it was always on me. I hated the whole thing.

GLORIA

You had no licenses, of course.

RICK

No.

GLORIA

This was a clear violation of Texas law 42.08.

RICK

A misdemeanor, yes.

GLORIA

Texas Penal Code 37.09 is a felony offense.

RICK

That's destroying evidence of a crime. There was no actual crime here!

GLORIA

That would come later.

A moment.

GLORIA

So you were comfortable with this?

RICK

Hell no! I was very fucking uncomfortable with it and I threatened to quit several times.

GLORIA

But you never did.

RICK

Because Richards had me over a barrel. This whole clusterfuck had happened on my watch, I was responsible, and he made it clear, without really saying it exactly, that they would hang me out to dry if I made a fuss.

GLORIA

But how bad could that be, Rick? I'm struggling to understand. As you yourself said, the situation was in some ways out of your control. They had overstuffed the facility despite your complaints. They hadn't provided you with the necessary medical staff or equipment that you had demanded. Why didn't you just quit and fight them in court if you had to?

RICK

(*Shaking his head*)

Historians. You guys always have the answer—after the fact. "Why didn't Napoleon turn left instead of right? If he had turned right, he would have won." Well, probably because he was in the middle of a fucking battle crapping his pants with shells going off all around him and people dying horribly. *You forget what it was like.* The country was fucking crazy. You were either, "with the government and the American people" or "against the government and the American people," and if you were against them, then maybe you ought to get over there with those illegals! And Stacey—

(*Gets emotional*)

—Stacey was expecting and the pregnancy was not going so well and my being away was hard enough as it was, I just didn't want to take the chance. I just. I just. I got them to promise to send me more medical supplies and to consider me for a transfer. Anywhere. It didn't matter, I would take anywhere, I just wanted to leave where I was as soon as possible.

GLORIA

That must have been incredibly hard for you with Stacey like that.

RICK

We were both really scared. The doctors were not optimistic.

GLORIA

And then Richards left. And you still had your problem.

RICK

Yes. At that point it was getting worse in fact.

GLORIA

That's where the factory came in.

A moment.

RICK

There was a blast furnace in this abandoned industrial complex nearby that was going to be decommissioned.

GLORIA

And you started burning the bodies there.

RICK

Yes.

GLORIA

You kept records of all this? Each person? Coroner's statement, cause of death, etcetera.

RICK

Initially, yes. Later, no.

GLORIA

Why not later?

RICK hesitates. His face colors.

RICK

We were—we were no longer pretending to—to follow the

normal, the normal rules. Richards said that, uh, that under the circumstances, we could just, just let that slide.

GLORIA

Record keeping. Specifically, mortality records.

RICK

Yes.

GLORIA

Paperwork was stamped "Deceased." Cause of death was "Illness." Then papers just stopped. And you say Richards sanctioned this?

RICK

Yes.

GLORIA

The prosecution made a lot of the fact that there was almost no correspondence, hard correspondence, between you and Richards. No letters. No memos. No emails. Not from his end, anyway, and not one on any of these key decision points like this.

RICK

They were always conversations, either by phone or in person. It was the only way I could get his attention.

GLORIA

Didn't you think that was unusual?

RICK

At first I didn't care, I was just glad to have somebody's attention. Some help. Later on, yeah, I thought, it was, odd. The
mortality record thing I just put down to ordinary productivity incentives.

GLORIA

"Productivity incentives?"

RICK

We were being paid by the body—

GLORIA

(*Gently correcting*)
The person.

A moment.

RICK

Right. Person. The government was paying us per person, to
hold and then process illegals.

GLORIA

Process meaning "repatriate."

RICK

Yes. So keeping the bodies on the books a little longer meant, you know, more money. And that was wrong,
I know, but I thought that money might free up some

additional resources and actually make things better for everybody. I get that's not exactly straight but my intentions were good.

A moment.

GLORIA

Later, "process" would mean something else.

A moment.

RICK

(*Very quietly*)

Yes.

GLORIA

How did you get to that?

RICK takes a drink of water.

RICK

It was during another visit with Richards. We were having some serious security issues.

GLORIA

There were riots.

RICK

I wouldn't go that far but yes, there were some demonstrations among the population and in one case, they injured two guards and an inmate was killed.

GLORIA
Why were they demonstrating?

RICK
(*Shrugging*)
Conditions were terrible. People were still sick. It was a nightmare.

GLORIA
So Richards came down again. What happened?

RICK
He was pissed. Not even a pretense of being concerned about me or anything. And he didn't come by himself this time. There were three guys with him, two of them claiming to be from Homeland Security and this third guy, Jameson, claiming to be a representative of the NSA.

GLORIA
The NSA.

RICK
I said that's what they claimed.

GLORIA
What makes you think they weren't who they said they were?

RICK

I don't know. Just a feeling. Maybe they were. The whole thing was so, I don't know, unsettling. They seemed like very wired-in guys. Dressed smart. Talked tough. Knew this person and that person. What was I going to do, card 'em? Clearly, they impressed the hell out of Richards because he was very, very careful around them. Very respectful. Like, you know, always checking their responses to what he said. Or didn't say.

GLORIA

And what did they say?

RICK

They said, they said the situation in the country had reached a crisis. We were in a war and we were losing. We had to be bold. Seize the moment. Show we weren't going to be pushed around. The pitch was very military. Very patriotic.

GLORIA

What did you understand the crisis to be?

RICK

We had all these people, you know, rounded all these people up, but we couldn't possibly repatriate them fast enough and we were getting dinged in the press by other countries criticizing us.

A moment.

GLORIA

When did you understand what they were saying?

RICK

The NSA guy, Jameson, said to me, "You need to make them go away." I said, "The detainees?" And he nodded. And then I laughed, I made a joke of it, I said, "Like what, kill them all?" I mean, I couldn't believe we were being serious here. But he didn't laugh. Nobody laughed. And Richards just looked away, his face all bloodless all of a sudden.

GLORIA

What did they say?

RICK

Nothing. They all just looked at me.

GLORIA

What did you say?

RICK

I said I couldn't do that.
    (*Beat*)
And then Jameson, the NSA guy, he took me by the arm and he pulled me away from the others and he started talking to me. Very quietly. He was a big guy. Tall. Very. Forceful. But quiet. I had a feeling about him, like he was maybe military once. Just something about the way he held himself.

He said, look, who do you think you are? You can't do this? You've already done this. People are dead. Under your watch. You've already broken half a dozen laws at least. I said, not like this. And he looked at me and he said, let me tell you something. My son. I gotta son, he's eleven now. When he was five, he had a brain tumor. A brain tumor, all right. Size of a tennis ball. That motherfucker was going to kill him. So the doctors said, this is what we've got to do. We are going to crack open his skull and cut out the tumor. Scoop it out like a rotten melon. And I said okay 'cause I wanted my son to live. So they did that. But it didn't work, it came back. And so then they zapped my son, my child, with huge doses of radiation. And that didn't work. The cancer came back. And so finally they dripped chemicals into his body. These chemicals were so toxic that the nurses who did the procedure? They had to wear special clothing and wear special masks just to handle it because it would burn their skin if they touched it but they were going to drip that shit into my boy's veins and that's what they did. And he screamed until he lost his voice and then he just wept and he asked me why I let them hurt him like that? He was a good boy. What had he done wrong? And all I could do was just hold him and pray a lot. And that's what I did. And he lived. He's cancer-free now. Aside from the scars on the top of his head which you can't really see, he's a normal kid, he loves baseball and is crazy about Pokémon and *he's OK*. And then Jameson put his arm around me and he said, this is the same thing, Rick. We got the same problem here. This country has a kind of rot inside and if we don't deal with it, it's going to kill us so we gotta take it out. It's not going to be pretty. But it's necessary. And then this car pulled up, government car, black sedan, and we got into it and we drove out to the factory.

GLORIA

Your factory?

RICK

(*Nodding*)

There were guys out there; a construction team. I didn't know any of 'em, hadn't seen them before. Jameson must have brought them in from somewhere else. They were just regular guys, you know, but they seemed to know what they were doing.

GLORIA

What were they doing?

RICK

They were retrofitting one of the large storage rooms in the factory maybe a hundred yards from the furnace area. Originally it was a low-ceiling brick room with a concrete floor and windows. They had bricked in the windows and replaced the original entrance doors with two large double steel doors.

(*Beat*)

There was a thick glass peephole in one of the doors. On

the other side of the room you had a very thick roll-down, roll-up steel door outside of which was a loading dock.

GLORIA

What else?

A moment.

RICK

They had enlarged the drains in the floor.

GLORIA

What else?

RICK

They added a large exhaust van in the ceiling and bricked in the windows on all sides but on the fourth side they added steel ducts.

GLORIA

Why?

RICK

Jameson explained to me that all you had to do was back a semi up and connect the exhaust pipe to the plumbing with flexible hoses. Very easy he said.
(*Beat*)
They also added two large water mains just outside the doors.

GLORIA

Water mains. Why?

RICK

So you could sluice the floors.

(*Beat*)

We ran a test that afternoon. A bus, windows blacked out, transported a group out from the stadium. They were told they were going to finally be processed and deported. They were relieved, you could see it on their faces. The bus pulls up and they were unloaded into the room and told to wait in line. They had painted lines on the floor, like at the airport when you fly in from another country. They lined up. Everybody was very obedient. The doors were closed. The semi started up. Whole thing took twenty minutes. Felt like forever. I went back to my office and threw up. I was shaking.

A moment.

GLORIA

What did your men call those transport buses? Later on? There was some kind of joke about that right?

RICK

I heard, uh, I heard some people call them taco trucks.

A moment.

GLORIA

Why didn't you stand up to them?

RICK takes a breath.

RICK

He never said it in so many words, Jameson, but he made it very clear that if I didn't approve—
  (*Gestures vaguely*)
And I thought about it. I did. But there was Stacey and the baby, our daughter had just been born a couple of weeks premature and she was having some difficulties. They weren't sure how serious. My family needed me. I had responsibilities. And even if I had made some kind of stand or something, so what? What difference would it have made? Somebody else would have just taken my place.

GLORIA

How did your staff take this?

RICK

Not everybody knew what was going on. We tried to keep it very—compartmentalized. But nobody who knew was happy. Nobody. There were—bonuses attached, which were substantial. But still, some guys were, were upset. You know. We talked about it. The company had a mental health counselor come out but people weren't sure if he was real or not so most of them didn't talk to him.

GLORIA

Real?

RICK

There was some idea he might be an informant. We were all pretty paranoid by that point.
(*Beat*)
Once they sent out a minister. This was after my administrative assistant, Janice, had a, a nervous breakdown, I guess.

GLORIA

What did the minister say?

RICK

He gave a sermon about Joshua killing the Canaanites. And he quoted Psalm 106.

GLORIA

Remind me.

RICK

(*Thinks a moment*)
"They did not destroy the people as the Lord commanded but they mixed with the nations and learned to do as they

did. Then the—the anger of the Lord was kindled against his people, and he abhorred his heritage; he gave them into the hand of the nations, so that those who hated them ruled over them."

(*Bitterly*)

I noticed he didn't stay on to watch the process.

GLORIA

(*Gently*)

How did you handle it?

RICK

After that first time, I never went back to the factory when they were, when they were operating. If there was a problem, I might go out there but mostly I stayed in the facility. I drank pretty heavily. I was also taking sedatives. Valium. Halcion. It was the only way I could sleep.

A moment.

GLORIA

Tell me about Esteban Gonzales. The young boy. I noticed you seemed very upset by his testimony at the trial.

RICK

(*Miserable*)

I liked that kid. I liked Esteban and I, I kept him safe, and then he said all that stuff about me at the trial.

GLORIA

How did you even notice him?

RICK

He was very, very personable. And smart. When he first arrived at the facility he stood out, made it clear he had skills.

GLORIA

Wood carving.

RICK

Yeah, for a fifteen-year-old he was really good.

GLORIA

What would he do?

RICK

He would make things to order for the guards and staff. Little stuff. Pins. Eagles were very popular. The flag. "Make America Great Again."

GLORIA

And you helped him out.

RICK

I made sure he had food. Medicine when he got sick. I kept him safe from the other prisoners.

GLORIA

What happened to his parents?

A moment.

RICK

I don't know.

GLORIA

Were they killed?

RICK

Probably.

GLORIA

He said he asked you many times and you told him not worry
about them.
(*Beat*)
And then somehow, this fifteen-year-old kid, somehow he
gets a hold of somebody's cell phone.

RICK

One of the guards', probably. Some dumb-ass, not thinking.

GLORIA

And Esteban, this kid, manages to take a picture and sends
it out and it goes viral and suddenly everybody is asking

questions and they come and they shut you down and arrest you.

> RICK

Yes.

> *A moment. GLORIA looks at her watch.*

> GLORIA

We probably only have a few minutes or so. I wanted to ask you something. It didn't really come up at the trial so much. The plane.

> RICK

The plane?

> GLORIA

Tell me about the plane.

> *RICK is silent.*

> GLORIA

You just said that after that first day, you never went back to the factory except when there was a problem. The implication was that the factory just ran on its own after that. Without you. But after a couple of weeks somebody went to a lot of trouble to move an old nonfunctioning airliner outside the factory to make it look more like an actual detention center. Like if you went through the processing there was the plane on the other side of the building that was going to take you home. Pretty effective tactic. Like wooden soap. Did you do that?

(*Beat*)

Nobody could have put that plane there, Rick, without your knowledge or your permission. I spoke to Esteban and he told me that it was your idea. He said he heard you talking about it. He said you were proud of it. He said you even made a little joke about it. He said you called it "Air America."

RICK looks shaken.

GLORIA

Why'd you do that, Rick? Put the plane there. Are you going to tell me that was a, a humanitarian gesture to, how did you put it earlier, "calm people down and reduce their anxiety—because it was the right thing to do?"

(*Bearing down*)

Or was it to make the operation even more *efficient*?

RICK says nothing.

GLORIA

At the trial there was disagreement about the actual number of people murdered at the factory. What do you think?

A moment.

RICK

I don't know. I heard, I heard twenty-five, twenty-six, twenty-seven.

GLORIA

Thousand.

RICK starts to weep.

GLORIA

When you finally told Stacey what you were charged with, what did she say? What did she say when she understood?

RICK

She, uh, she cried. And she wouldn't—*look* at me. For a long time.

(*Beat*)

She's good about visiting me and stuff but—she still doesn't really look at me.

GLORIA

Why did this happen, Rick? Help us understand.

A moment.

RICK

I had a dream in here. Nightmare, I guess. Woke me straight up in the middle of the night in a cold sweat. Shaking like detox. Nightmare's not the right word. Revelation? The president said he was going to build a wall, a beautiful wall, and he would make Mexico pay for it. And everybody laughed at that, all you smart people laughed at that because of course, it's absurd. You can't really build a wall that big and that high to keep people out if they really want to get in. And Mexico was never going to pay for any of that shit. But that's not what he meant. See. That was the revelation. It wasn't a real wall, a brick and mortar wall. That wasn't what he was talking about. What is a wall? It's a, a construct, a, a device, for keeping people out. What we built was so much more effective. It will keep people out for years because nobody will want to come here now.

Fade to black.

Afterwords

Breaking Down

by Timothy Patrick McCarthy

America is in the midst of a breakdown.

All around us, the sad casualties: rule of law, trust in institutions, democratic governance, checks and balances, the common good. And don't get me started about liberty, equality, rights, and the pursuit of happiness, which are all supposedly "founding" ideals. These self-evident truths—indeed, truth itself—are under assault by people who know something about assault and nothing about truth. We are living in a dystopian, absurdist version of our national self. And there's nothing "great" about any of this.

#RealTruth: Art sustains us through the best of times and the worst of times.

As a historian, I know we've been here before, again and again. But history can be a muse and a guide. Robert Schenkkan is one of those great American artists who has always used history as a muse and guide—and to great effect.

He first won the Pulitzer Prize for telling the nation's story when I was still in college studying American history and literature, long before I became a storyteller myself.

Since 9/11—one of those watershed moments in American history that has shaped and silenced the stories we tell—I have taught a course at Harvard called "American Protest Literature from Tom Paine to Tupac." It was one of the first of its kind in the nation. As the title suggests, it's a capacious course, one that "contains multitudes," as Walt Whitman, one of the many authors we read, suggests. Those who seek to sustain the status quo often disparage protest art as "propaganda," when, in fact, it is the opposite: it disrupts the intentions and impositions of state power and those who seek to justify or defend it. When I think of those great works of American protest literature—Tom Paine's *Common Sense*, David Walker's *Appeal*, Harriet Beecher Stowe's *Uncle Tom's Cabin*, Ida B. Wells-Barnett's *Southern Horrors*, John Steinbeck's *Grapes of Wrath*, Betty Friedan's *Feminine Mystique*, Dr. Martin Luther King, Jr.'s *Letter from Birmingham Jail*, James Baldwin's *The Fire Next Time*, Tony Kushner's *Angels in America*, among so many others—I do not see artists in service to the state. On the contrary, I see courageous citizens, and those who aspire to full citizenship, who have used their creative gifts to critique the powers that be, to create a countervailing story of the nation, and to call for a new kind of world. Frankly, America would have died long ago if not for these democratic dissenters.

At its best, protest art functions in three ways. First, it

shocks us into recognition. If we encounter the world around us from a place of ignorance or indifference, we need someone to awaken us and provoke us. Such confrontation raises our consciousness, whether we like it or not. Second, protest art *calls us to empathy*. If we only recognize or acknowledge the people who are just like us, we need something outside of ourselves to help us understand what it's like to walk in another person's shoes or live in another person's skin. This is perhaps the most difficult thing to do, but also the most important. Third, protest art *invites us into conversation*. Not all protest art tells us exactly what to do, even if it calls on us to do something. The best protest literature models what Kenneth Burke called "symbolic action," the rich ambiguity in any given text that inspires robust debate and encourages different interpretations. Protest art breaks us down by breaking apart the things we think we knew and breaking us free to imagine alternatives. But it also builds us up, not beyond or between or behind walls, but into new communities that embrace and nurture our full humanity.

Theater plays a special role in all of this. There are precious few art forms that are so intimate and immediate, different each time than it was the last time. The experience of theater-going is collective and the process of theater-making is collaborative. We watch it and work on it together. The best theater also inspires us to break down the walls that sometimes separate us—the "fourth wall," of course, but so many other walls as well. There has scarcely been a time in our history when theater—and art in all its forms—has been more relevant, more important, and more urgent. It is time, again, to use art to break down every last wall we see, to build our broken selves into a better nation and a bigger world. Let's get to work!

Timothy Patrick McCarthy is an award-winning scholar, educator, and activist. He holds a joint faculty appointment at Harvard University, where he is Director of Culture Change & Social Justice Initiatives at the Carr Center for Human Rights Policy at the John F. Kennedy School of Government. The author or editor of four books from the New Press, including The Radical Reader *and* Prophets of Protest, *Dr. McCarthy is the host and director of* The A.R.T. of Human Rights, *an ongoing public conversation series on art and politics co-sponsored by the Carr Center and at the American Repertory Theater.*

The Real Purpose
of the Border Wall

by Douglas S. Massey

Donald Trump's call for the construction of a continuous
wall along the Mexico-US border has little to do with the
control of immigration and everything to do with the symbolic politics of white nationalism. The border is already the
most secure international boundary anywhere in the world,
with the possible exception of the frontier between the two
Koreas. It is defended by a Border Patrol of 21,000 agents
with an annual budget of \$3.7 billion, making it the largest
arms-bearing branch of the federal government except for
the military itself.

The irony is that illegal migration ended nine years ago
and has been net zero or negative ever since. Apprehensions
along the border are at their lowest level since 1971, when
the Border Patrol had a force of just 1,550 officers and a
budget of only \$56 million. Undocumented immigration
from Mexico actually began to decline around the year 2000,

and it came to an abrupt halt during the Great Recession of 2008. Although a small number of Central Americans continue to seek entry at the border, more undocumented Mexicans go home each year than enter the United States. As a result, the size of the undocumented population has not increased for a decade—and this is according to the US Department of Homeland Security's own estimates.

Contrary to what immigration hard-liners argue, the end of illegal migration has nothing to do with border enforcement. If anything, the massive increase in the enforcement effort between 1986 and 2006 was counterproductive. Studies show that it had no effect on the likelihood that a Mexican would depart for the United States without documents or successfully cross the border into the United States. However, the militarization of the border *did* increase the costs and risks of undocumented entry, raising smuggler fees from around $500 per crossing before 1990 to around $4,500 today and increasing the number of migrant deaths from 67 in 1993 to 492 in 2005.

In response to these rising costs and risks, undocumented migrants quite naturally minimized border crossing—not by remaining in Mexico but by staying in the United States once they had paid the costs and experienced the risks at the border. Prior to 1986, 85 percent of annual unauthorized entries were offset by departures and the undocumented population grew slowly. After that date, the rate of return migration fell rapidly as migrants stopped circulating to avoid the need for border crossing. As a result, the massive expansion of border enforcement paradoxically *increased* net undocumented migration, driving out-migration down while having no discernable effect on in-migration and thereby *doubling* the rate of undocumented population growth.

In the end, undocumented migration ultimately fell to net zero because of Mexico's demographic transition, as the nation shifted from a fertility rate of seven children per woman in the 1960s to a figure of around 2.2 children per woman today. Given this drop in the birth rate, the number of people entering the labor force ages (from eighteen to sixty-four) was plunging by the turn of the century, and at this point Mexico has turned a corner to become a rapidly aging society.

The rate of migration follows a very clear age pattern, rising from sixteen to peak in the early twenties and then declining rapidly to low levels by age thirty. If one does not begin migrating between the ages of sixteen and thirty, one is very unlikely to begin migrating at all—and the average age in Mexico is now twenty-eight. Undocumented migration ceased because the number of people in the migrant-prone ages fell sharply and age-eligible candidates for international migration are now quite scarce.

If border enforcement was counterproductive in the first place and illegal migration has been zero or negative for nine years, why has Trump issued an executive order calling for the completion of a two-thousand-mile border wall? The answer is simple: it is a symbolic gesture to placate his resentful white political base. A border wall cannot lower undocumented migration because it is already zero; but it does send a clear signal to supporters that Mexico and Mexicans are a threat to the nation, Latino immigrants are unfit for inclusion in US society, and our neighbors to the south are not and will never be accepted as "real Americans." Trump's proposal for a wall is all about the symbolic politics of race. Indeed, the wall may never be erected given its estimated price tag of $22 billion; but in signing the executive order, Trump has already achieved his principal purpose of pandering to anti-Latino prejudice and burnishing his white nationalist credentials for his alt-right supporters.

Douglas S. Massey is the Henry G. Bryant Professor of Sociology and Public Affairs at Princeton University and Director of its Office of Population Research.

The Darkness within Our Historical Walls

by Julian E. Zelizer

Americans like to think of our country as being exceptional. We rightly point to the many virtuous aspects of our past—our commitment to constant elections, our growing embrace of social justice and human rights, our willingness to protect individual liberties while preserving the constitutional system of checks and balances that stifles the most power-hungry of our elected officials. The belief in American Exceptionalism is shared by liberals and conservatives. When the courts pushed back on President Trump's executive order on banning refugees from seven countries, there were many citizens who praised the decision as evidence of the ability of our system to work.

Yet in our celebration of the past, we too often overlook the darker sides of our political tradition. Other elements of our political development reveal powerful reactionary forces that have also continually shaped the polity.

These forces of discord, division, and repression are not anomalies and aberrations. Rather, they are as American as apple pie.

Five decades of historical scholarship since the 1960s have shown how liberal values frequently lose out in public policy. Indeed, xenophobia, nativism, and racism have often converged and formed a potent mix in our treatment of immigrants and refugees, as we have been seeing play out in recent months under the Trump presidency.

Nativism and xenophobia are nothing new. Although this country was founded by immigrants and built around a perpetual flow of people entering from other nations, each wave of newcomers has usually produced a strong counter-movement of restriction. This was evident in 1882 when the Chinese Exclusion Act prohibited the immigration of Chinese workers. In 1924, after a long period of massive immigration from Eastern and Southern Europe, Congress passed legislation that imposed national origins quotas preventing any more newcomers from arriving to our shores. When Jewish refugees from the Nazi genocide attempted to enter into the United States, hostile elements in the State Department blocked their admission. In recent years, immigrants have been the focus of legislative attack in states such as California and Arizona, where hard-line conservative elements have clamped down on the rights of those who are here by illegal as well as legal means. In Congress, proposals to create a path for citizenship have been stifled by a large bloc in the GOP.

The anger toward immigrants has expressed itself at times beyond legislation and regulatory policy. During the 1910s and 1920s, the pseudoscientific field of eugenics gained national respectability by offering a means for government officials to allegedly measure the intelligence of members of different ethnic groups, categorizing them on a sliding scale of value.

The political drive behind this nativist energy has been varied. To be sure, there have been Americans whose major concern has been about jobs. In moments of economic hardship and in communities that are suffering even in boom times, the fear of the immigrant has often been shaped by concerns that people arriving to the United States would take much-needed jobs away from people already living here. This was the justification in 1954 when the Immigration and Nationalization Service launched "Operation Wetback," which cracked down on illegal immigration from Mexico.

But racism has usually been the strongest motivation for the campaigns around imposing punitive policies. American political history has been replete with intense social animosity that leads Americans to see immigrants as being the "other"—inferior, dangerous, and undesirable. Almost each new immigrant group has experienced some kind of racial hostility, even those, such as the Irish and Eastern European Jews, who were eventually able to integrate into mainstream social life.

The restrictionist tradition has often succeeded by connecting immigration to the theme of national security.

Threats to the nation, some real and some imagined, become the crisis framework used to justify punitive action that supports the nativist cause. Most famously, in 1942, Franklin Roosevelt issued an executive order creating internment camps for Japanese Americans based on concerns about threats stemming from World War II. The Immigration and Nationality Act of 1952, which the Trump administration has used as the legal justification for their executive order, authorized the government to deport immigrants and naturalized citizens who were accused of engaging in subversive actions and to prevent them from entering into the United States as well. Despite President Truman's veto of the bill, Congress passed the measure as being necessary to fight communism.

In the American polity, the strength of the reactionary element of our political tradition does wax and wane. In 1965, when Congress passed a major immigration reform bill that ended the national quota system, the values of civil rights triumphed over the legacy of xenophobia. But there are moments when reactionary forces seem quite powerful, able to shape an entire political campaign or have important effects on lasting public policies. While we want to push aside these parts of our tradition with the belief that things will be better in the future, history shows that this is a mistake. The right mix of political actors, national security crises, and hard-line social movements has always been able to thrust our reactionary national genetics to the very center of our political debate and inscribe those values into social policy. When that occurs, we have been at our worst as a nation.

Julian E. Zelizer is a political historian at Princeton University and a fellow at New America. He is also a contributor to CNN, where he writes a weekly column and appears as a regular guest on television. His most recent book is The Fierce Urgency of Now: Lyndon Johnson, Congress, and the Battle for the Great Society *(Penguin Press).*